TAGAKI
多書き

TAGAKI（多書き）とは、一言で言えば、「英語で自分を表現することを学ぶための、ボルダリング競技みたいなもの」です。その足場はメンタル面と英語面の2種類で、この足場を使って登って行き頂上を目指しましょう。このTAGAKIでは、考える→書く→伝えるを30トピック繰り返すことで、自分の意見を持ち、英語を書けるようになります。そうすると世界に飛び出して行けそうな自分を感じることができるでしょう。

TAGAKI 40 Contents もくじ

| | このワークブックの進め方 | | 4 |

Topics   **Categories**

#		Topic	Category	Page
1	World	April Fool's Day (エイプリルフール)	Culture	6
2	Japan	Bento (弁当)	Culture	8
3	Japan	Commuting by Train (電車通学／通勤)	Life	10
4	World	Dogs (犬)	Living Things	12
5	Japan	Fireworks (花火大会)	Culture	14
6	Japan	Freshmen (新入生)	Life	16
7	World	Going to School on Foot (徒歩通学)	Life	18
8	Japan	Hiroshima (広島)	Places	20
9	Japan	Hot Spring Manners (温泉のマナー)	Culture	22
10	World	Housework (家事)	Life	24
11	Japan	Karate (空手)	Sport	26
12	Japan	Kendo (剣道)	Sport	28
13	World	Loch Ness Monster (ネッシー)	Mystery	30
14	Japan	Manzai Performers (漫才師)	Entertainment	32
15	World	Marie Antoinette (マリー・アントワネット)	History	34
16	World	Mayonnaise (マヨネーズ)	Food	36
17	World	Mermaids (人魚)	Mystery	38
18	World	Modern Art Museums (現代美術館)	Art	40
19	World	Movies (映画)	Entertainment	42
20	Japan	Mount Fuji (富士山)	Places	44
21	Japan	Pollen Allergies (花粉症)	Seasons	46

22	●World ▶ **Ramen** (ラーメン)	Food	48
23	●Japan ▶ **Rhinoceros Beetles and Stag Beetles** (カブトムシとクワガタムシ)	Living Things	50
24	●Japan ▶ **Rice Balls** (おにぎり)	Food	52
25	●Japan ▶ **Shopping Malls** (ショッピングモール)	Places	54
26	●Japan ▶ **Snow** (雪)	Nature	56
27	●Japan ▶ **Takoyaki** (たこ焼き)	Food	58
28	●Japan ▶ **Toki** (トキ)	Living Things	60
29	●World ▶ **Tutankhamen** (ツタンカーメン)	History	62
30	●World ▶ **Van Gogh** (ゴッホ)	Art	64

進度表 終わったトピックの番号に印をつけていきましょう!

TAGAKI 40 をはじめよう

自分のオリジナル文を入れて書きます。創造性（creativity）を発揮し楽しく羽ばたいてみましょう。国際的には自分のオリジナリティがあることが大切になってきますので、他の人と違うことを考えてみましょう。また「伝える」ところで、学習者同士が発表し合えたらどんなに楽しいかわくわくしてきますね。

進め方

文の構成

- **Catchy Sentences（つかみ）**　これからこのような話をすると、端的に相手にわからせ、ひきつけることを書きます。
- **Facts（事実）**　つかみを裏付ける説明や事実関係、理由などを書きます。
- **Punch Lines（おち）**　話のしめくくりになることを書きます。

Step 1 （Thinking / Reading）

トピックについて考えましょう。**Sample Sentences** の **Catchy Sentence** を読んで、テーマを読み取ります。次に **Facts** のリード文を読み、自分のオリジナル文を2文考えます。

Step 2 （Listening）

Sample Sentences と **Hints for Original Sentences** の音声をQRコードできくことができます。音声をチェックしましょう。

考える

1人でTAGAKIを学ぶ人へ

単独の良さをいかし、自由に自分のペースでStep1〜5を進めてください。自分で自分の進歩を見届け、それぞれの目的や目標、例えば入試や検定試験、会議やプレゼンなどのために書く力を付けてください。

TAGAKI 40 目標

メンタル 自分の創造性をアピールする

国際的には、自分のオリジナリティがあることが大切です。他人と違うことを言ったり、考えたり、表現したりして、自分なりの独創性を発揮しましょう。

英語 自分のオリジナルな2文を含め、40語前後の英文を書く

4つのヒントを参考に、ユニークでおもしろいことや冗談、他人がはっとするようなことを、自分のオリジナルの文で表現しましょう。初めは、ヒントを利用して書き写しても構いません。

書く 5〜7分で書きましょう。

Step 3

Hints for Original Sentences を参考にして、Facts に自分のオリジナル文を2文加え、全文を書き写しましょう。初めのうちは、写しても構いませんが、徐々に自分のオリジナル文を書けるようにしましょう。

Step 4

Writing Time 1 で書いた文を見ないで、もう一度書きましょう。

伝える

Step 5

Writing Time 2 で書いた文を覚えて声に出して言いましょう。

ペアやグループでTAGAKIを学ぶ人へ

Step1〜5を進めた後、友達や家族、先生に向けて発表したり、他の人の発表を聞いて、英語または日本語でディスカッションしたりして、4技能の学習へ発展してください。書いたものは見ないで発表しましょう。

Culture 〈文化〉
April Fool's Day
エイプリルフール

音声がきけます♪

Sample Sentences

Catchy Sentences
April 1st is April Fool's Day. On that day, you're allowed to tell a lie before noon.

Facts
Here're some lies you might want to tell.

1. Original Sentences
2. Original Sentences

Punch Lines
Liar, liar, pants on fire!

Hints for Original Sentences

❶ I found a snake in my house!

❷ My dad won the lottery!

❸ Mount Everest has erupted!

❹ An alien was caught by the police!

Writing Time

1 エイプリルフールの日についてみたいうそを2つ考えて ① と ② に文を入れて、全文を書こう。

- Catchy Sentences
- Facts
- Punch Lines

2 上で書いた文を見ないで書いて、見ないで言おう。

- Catchy Sentences
- Facts
- Punch Lines

Culture 〈文化〉

Bento
弁当

Sample Sentences

Catchy Sentences: Bento is a must for Japanese people. And homemade bento is special.

Facts: Here're some important rules for homemade bento.

① Original Sentences

② Original Sentences

Punch Lines: My mom's bento is the best!

bento … boxed lunch

Hints for Original Sentences

❶ You must make it colorful.

❷ You must make it healthy.

❸ You must make it very big/small.

❹ You must make it decorative.

8

Writing Time

1 手作り弁当で大切なことを 2 つ考えて ① と ② に文を入れて、全文を書こう。

Catchy Sentences

Facts

Punch Lines

2 上で書いた文を見ないで書いて、見ないで言おう。

Catchy Sentences

Facts

Punch Lines

3 Japan

Life 〈生活・人生〉

Commuting by Train

電車通学／通勤

 音声がきけます♪

Sample Sentences

Catchy Sentences
In Japan, many people commute to offices and schools by train.

Facts
Here're some good things about commuting by train.

① Original Sentences

② Original Sentences

Punch Lines
I love people watching, too.

Hints for Original Sentences

① Trains are usually on time.

② People get a chance to take a nap.

③ People can check their mobile phones.

④ Students can do their homework.

10

Writing Time

1 電車通学や通勤の良い点を2つ考えて ① と ② に文を入れて、全文を書こう。

- Catchy Sentences
- Facts
- Punch Lines

2 上で書いた文を見ないで書いて、見ないで言おう。

- Catchy Sentences
- Facts
- Punch Lines

4 Living Things 〈生きもの〉

Dogs
犬

音声がきけます♪

Sample Sentences

Catchy Sentences: Dogs do funny things all the time. The owners sometimes get mad at their dogs.

Facts: Here're two things that "bad" dogs sometimes do.

① Original Sentences

② Original Sentences

Punch Lines: But I still love them.

Hints for Original Sentences

❶ They eat everybody's slippers.

❷ They chase the neighbor's cat.

❸ They chew cardboard boxes.

❹ They make a big mess.

Writing Time

1 行儀が悪い犬がしそうなことを2つ考えて ① と ② に文を入れて、全文を書こう。

Catchy Sentences

Facts

Punch Lines

2 上で書いた文を見ないで書いて、見ないで言おう。

Catchy Sentences

Facts

Punch Lines

Culture 〈文化〉

Fireworks
花火大会

音声がきけます♪

Sample Sentences

Catchy Sentences: In many different times and places, men and women, young and old, have loved fireworks.

Facts: Here're some suggestions for when you go to a fireworks festival.

① Original Sentences

② Original Sentences

Punch Lines: Fireworks over water are especially beautiful.

Hints for Original Sentences

❶ You eat shaved ice and takoyaki.

❷ You wear a yukata.

❸ You bring a picnic sheet to sit on.

❹ You bring an umbrella in case of rain.

Writing Time

1 花火大会に行く時の良いアイデアを 2 つ考えて ① と ② に文を入れて、全文を書こう。

Catchy Sentences

Facts

Punch Lines

2 上で書いた文を見ないで書いて、見ないで言おう。

Catchy Sentences

Facts

Punch Lines

Life 〈生活・人生〉

Freshmen
新入生

Sample Sentences

Catchy Sentences
April is a special month in Japan. It's the beginning of the year in schools and companies.

Facts
Here're some things that freshmen often say.

1 Original Sentences

2 Original Sentences

Punch Lines
Welcome freshmen!

Hints for Original Sentences

❶ I'll study/work hard.

❷ I'll get up early.

❸ I'll make many friends.

❹ I'll change my hairstyle.

16

Writing Time

1 新入生がよく言うことを2つ考えて ① と ② に文を入れて、全文を書こう。

- Catchy Sentences
- Facts
- Punch Lines

2 上で書いた文を見ないで書いて、見ないで言おう。

- Catchy Sentences
- Facts
- Punch Lines

Life 〈生活・人生〉

Going to School on Foot
徒歩通学

音声がきけます♪

Sample Sentences

Catchy Sentences

Many children in the world walk to school.

It's an important part of some children's lives to walk to school with their friends.

Facts

Here're some good points about walking to school.

① Original Sentences

② Original Sentences

Punch Lines

Don't be silly! Don't be late!

Hints for Original Sentences

❶ The children make friends.

❷ The children enjoy going to school together.

❸ The children learn social rules and manners.

❹ Walking is good for the children's health.

Writing Time

1 徒歩通学の良い点を2つ考えて ① と ② に文を入れて、全文を書こう。

Catchy Sentences

Facts

Punch Lines

2 上で書いた文を見ないで書いて、見ないで言おう。

Catchy Sentences

Facts

Punch Lines

Places 〈場所〉

Hiroshima
広島

音声がきけます♪

Sample Sentences

Catchy Sentences: A visit to Hiroshima will be a great experience for visitors from foreign countries, as well as Japanese people of all ages.

Facts: If you go to Hiroshima, here're some suggestions.
① Original Sentences
② Original Sentences

Punch Lines: "No more nuclear weapons!" is our wish.

Hints for Original Sentences

❶ You visit the Hiroshima Peace Memorial Museum.

❷ You visit the Atomic Bomb Dome.

❸ You attend the memorial ceremony on August 6th.

❹ You participate in the guided tour by survivors.

Writing Time

1 広島へ行くなら見逃すべきではないものを2つ考えて ① と ② に文を入れて、全文を書こう。

Catchy Sentences

Facts

Punch Lines

2 上で書いた文を見ないで書いて、見ないで言おう。

Catchy Sentences

Facts

Punch Lines

Culture 〈文化〉

9 Hot Spring Manners
温泉のマナー

Sample Sentences

Catchy Sentences
Foreign guests are welcome at Japanese hot springs.

But there're a few rules they need to know.

Facts
1️⃣ Original Sentences

2️⃣ Original Sentences

Punch Lines
Aaaaaaah! That feels sooooo goooooood!

Hints for Original Sentences

❶ Swim suits aren't allowed.

❷ Wash your body before you get into the hot water.

❸ Don't put your towel in the hot water.

❹ Don't make too much noise.

TAGAKI 40

Writing Time

1 外国人観光客が知る必要がある入浴ルールを2つ考えて ① と ② に文を入れて、全文を書こう。

Catchy Sentences

Facts

Punch Lines

2 上で書いた文を見ないで書いて、見ないで言おう。

Catchy Sentences

Facts

Punch Lines

Life 〈生活・人生〉
Housework
家事

Sample Sentences

Catchy Sentences: Of all the housework, some people say the laundry is the easiest.

Facts: If you're asked to do chores, you might choose the laundry. Here're two reasons.

① Original Sentences

② Original Sentences

Punch Lines: Make sure you check all the pockets before doing the washing!

Hints for Original Sentences

❶ It's really easy. The machine does everything.

❷ You can play with your mobile phone while you wait.

❸ Freshly dried clothes smell so good.

❹ You can watch TV while you fold the washed clothes.

Writing Time

1 家事を頼まれたら洗濯を選ぶ理由を2つ考えて ① と ② に文を入れて、全文を書こう。

Catchy Sentences

Facts

Punch Lines

2 上で書いた文を見ないで書いて、見ないで言おう。

Catchy Sentences

Facts

Punch Lines

Sport 〈スポーツ〉

Karate
空手

Sample Sentences

Catchy Sentences
If you have a karate black belt, you have to register with the police. Well, that's NOT true!

Facts
Here're some common images people have of karate practitioners.

① Original Sentences

② Original Sentences

Punch Lines
Yahhhhhh!

Hints for Original Sentences

❶ They have strong voices.

❷ They all look fit.

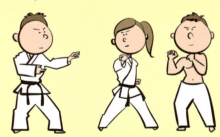

❸ They can break bricks with their hands.

❹ They can protect weak people very quickly.

26

Writing Time

1 空手家のイメージを2つ考えて ① と ② に文を入れて、全文を書こう。

Catchy Sentences

Facts

Punch Lines

2 上で書いた文を見ないで書いて、見ないで言おう。

Catchy Sentences

Facts

Punch Lines

Sport 〈スポーツ〉

Kendo
けんどう
剣道

音声がきけます♪

Sample Sentences

Catchy Sentences
Kendo is a popular sport nowadays, but it's hard to judge a kendo match.

Facts
Here're two reasons.
① Original Sentences
② Original Sentences

Punch Lines
Blink and you'll miss it!

Hints for Original Sentences

❶ It's too fast to judge.

❷ The rules are complicated.

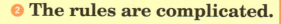

❸ There're three judges for a match, but that's not enough. It's still hard to judge.

❹ Both fighters hit each other many times.

Writing Time

1 剣道の試合の判定が難しい理由を2つ考えて ① と ② に文を入れて、全文を書こう。

Catchy Sentences

Facts

Punch Lines

2 上で書いた文を見ないで書いて、見ないで言おう。

Catchy Sentences

Facts

Punch Lines

Mystery 〈ミステリー〉
Loch Ness Monster
ネッシー

音声がきけます♪

Sample Sentences

Catchy Sentences: In 1933, a couple claimed they saw a monster in Loch Ness, a lake in Scotland, but it was only a joke!

Facts: Personally,

1. Original Sentences

2. Original Sentences

Punch Lines: Thousands of people have believed the joke!

Hints for Original Sentences

❶ I wanted to go to Scotland to see Nessie!

❷ I've seen a picture of Nessie.

❸ I think the joke was very well made.

❹ I think the joke made the lake a famous place.

TAGAKI 40

Writing Time

1 ネッシーの目撃(もくげき)についてどう思ったか2つ考えて ① と ② に文を入れて、全文を書こう。

- Catchy Sentences
- Facts
- Punch Lines

2 上で書いた文を見ないで書いて、見ないで言おう。

- Catchy Sentences
- Facts
- Punch Lines

31

Entertainment 〈娯楽〉

Manzai Performers
漫才師

Sample Sentences

Catchy Sentences
Many Japanese young people yearn to be Manzai performers. They perform funny talks in pairs. Actually, it's a very hard job. Here're two reasons.

Facts
1 Original Sentences

2 Original Sentences

Punch Lines
Everyone loves a good joke!

Hints for Original Sentences

① They must write their own scripts.

② They must practice a lot.

③ It's hard to make people laugh all the time.

④ They don't get paid if they aren't funny.

TAGAKI 40

Writing Time

1 漫才師(まんざいし)が大変な職業である理由を2つ考えて ① と ② に文を入れて、全文を書こう。

Catchy Sentences

Facts

Punch Lines

2 上で書いた文を見ないで書いて、見ないで言おう。

Catchy Sentences

Facts

Punch Lines

History 〈歴史〉

Marie Antoinette
マリー・アントワネット

Sample Sentences

Catchy Sentences / Facts: I'll interview Marie Antoinette, of France. When she was only 14 years old, she was sent to France from Austria to marry the future king Louis XVI. Here're my questions.

① Original Sentences

② Original Sentences

Punch Lines: She was executed by guillotine in 1793 during the French Revolution.

Hints for Original Sentences

❶ Did you really say, "Let them eat cake"?

❷ Why did the French Revolution happen?

❸ Were you the most tragic queen in history?

❹ Were the wigs heavy?

Writing Time

1 マリー・アントワネットに質問してみたいことを2つ考えて ① と ② に文を入れて、全文を書こう。

Catchy Sentences

Facts

Punch Lines

2 上で書いた文を見ないで書いて、見ないで言おう。

Catchy Sentences

Facts

Punch Lines

Food 〈食べもの〉

Mayonnaise
マヨネーズ

音声がきけます♪

Sample Sentences

Catchy Sentences: A short name for mayonnaise is "mayo." It's nice and short, isn't it?

Facts: As you all know, potato salad without mayonnaise is just not right. Here're some suggestions for enjoying mayonnaise more.

① Original Sentences

② Original Sentences

Punch Lines: No mayonnaise, no life!

Hints for Original Sentences

❶ You put mayonnaise on top of takoyaki.

❷ You dress asparagus with mayonnaise.

❸ You put mayonnaise on French fries.

❹ You put mayonnaise and soy sauce on top of rice.

Writing Time

1 マヨネーズがあるとよりおいしくなる食べものを2つ考えて ① と ② に文を入れて、全文を書こう。

Catchy Sentences

Facts

Punch Lines

2 上で書いた文を見ないで書いて、見ないで言おう。

Catchy Sentences

Facts

Punch Lines

Mystery 〈ミステリー〉

Mermaids
人魚

Sample Sentences

Catchy Sentences: The famous statue of the Little Mermaid is in Copenhagen, Denmark. The statue was based on one of Hans Christian Andersen's fairy tales.

Facts: Here're some commonly said things about mermaids.

1 Original Sentences

2 Original Sentences

Punch Lines: Someday, someone might see a real mermaid!

Hints for Original Sentences

❶ Mermaids are half human and half fish.

❷ Mermaids are actually dugongs.

❸ The Little Mermaid fell in love with Prince Charming.

❹ Mermaids are really good singers.

38

Writing Time

1 人魚についてよく知られていることを2つ考えて ① と ② に文を入れて、全文を書こう。

Catchy Sentences

Facts

Punch Lines

2 上で書いた文を見ないで書いて、見ないで言おう。

Catchy Sentences

Facts

Punch Lines

Art 〈芸術〉

Modern Art Museums
現代美術館

 音声がきけます♪

Sample Sentences

Catchy Sentences: Everybody sees something different in modern art. It's like finding shapes in clouds.

Facts: Here're two important things you need to keep in mind when you go to a modern art museum.

① Original Sentences

② Original Sentences

Punch Lines: Why don't we try?

Hints for Original Sentences

❶ You only need to feel something.

❷ You don't have to understand the work.

❸ You might find something you really like.

❹ You'd better take a small notebook to write down the artists' names. Someday, they might become famous.

TAGAKI 40

Writing Time

1 現代美術館に行く時に覚えておくべき大切なことを2つ考えて ① と ② に文を入れて、全文を書こう。

Catchy Sentences

Facts

Punch Lines

2 上で書いた文を見ないで書いて、見ないで言おう。

Catchy Sentences

Facts

Punch Lines

Entertainment 〈娯楽〉

Movies
映画

Sample Sentences

Catchy Sentences ▶ People around the world love movies. Why is that?

Facts ▶ Movies are just like time machines. They can take you to a different time and place. Here're some reasons why people like movies so much.

① Original Sentences

② Original Sentences

Punch Lines ▶ After two hours, you might feel different.

Hints for Original Sentences

❶ They want to see their favorite actors.

❷ They want to be just like their heroes.

❸ They want to enjoy good music and dance.

❹ They want to see remakes of famous stories.

Writing Time

1 みんなが映画を大好きな理由を2つ考えて ① と ② に文を入れて、全文を書こう。

- Catchy Sentences
- Facts
- Punch Lines

2 上で書いた文を見ないで書いて、見ないで言おう。

- Catchy Sentences
- Facts
- Punch Lines

Places 〈場所〉

Mount Fuji
富士山

音声がきけます♪

Sample Sentences

Catchy Sentences
Mount Fuji is one of the most famous mountains in the world.

Facts
There're a few things you'd better know before you actually climb it.

① Original Sentences

② Original Sentences

Punch Lines
You can even see nice drawings of Mount Fuji in many public baths.

Hints for Original Sentences

❶ Mount Fuji is 3,776 meters high.

❷ Mount Fuji is a sacred mountain.

❸ You must start climbing at night to see the beautiful sunrise.

❹ You can climb it from early July to early September.

44

Writing Time

1 富士山に登る前に知っておいたほうが良いことを 2 つ考えて ① と ② に文を入れて、全文を書こう。

Catchy Sentences

Facts

Punch Lines

2 上で書いた文を見ないで書いて、見ないで言おう。

Catchy Sentences

Facts

Punch Lines

Seasons 〈季節〉

Pollen Allergies
花粉症(かふんしょう)

音声がきけます♪

Sample Sentences

Catchy Sentences
Spring is a great season. But it's the season for pollen allergies, too! Many Japanese people suffer from them.

Facts
If you suffer from pollen allergies, you'll get some of the symptoms below.

① Original Sentences

② Original Sentences

Punch Lines
Go away pollen allergies! AaaaaAAACHOO!

pollen allergies … hay fever

Hints for Original Sentences

❶ You can't stop sneezing.

❷ You get a runny nose.

❸ You get a headache.

❹ You get itchy eyes.

Writing Time

1 花粉症の症状を2つ考えて ① と ② に文を入れて、全文を書こう。

Catchy Sentences

Facts

Punch Lines

2 上で書いた文を見ないで書いて、見ないで言おう。

Catchy Sentences

Facts

Punch Lines

Food 〈食べもの〉

Ramen
ラーメン

Sample Sentences

Catchy Sentences: Ramen is so good! It's an international food nowadays.

Facts: You can find ramen shops in almost any part of the world. Here're two reasons why ramen is popular.

① Original Sentences

② Original Sentences

Punch Lines: Without ramen, the world will end!

Hints for Original Sentences

❶ You can choose from different soup tastes.

❷ It gives you instant satisfaction.

❸ Each ramen shop offers their own original ramen.

❹ Ramen tastes better if you eat it with your friends.

Writing Time

1 ラーメンが人気の理由を 2 つ考えて ① と ② に文を入れて、全文を書こう。

Catchy Sentences

Facts

Punch Lines

2 上で書いた文を見ないで書いて、見ないで言おう。

Catchy Sentences

Facts

Punch Lines

Living Things 〈生きもの〉

Rhinoceros Beetles and Stag Beetles
カブトムシとクワガタムシ

音声がきけます♪

Sample Sentences

Catchy Sentences
Japanese children, especially boys, love rhinoceros beetles and stag beetles. Why do boys like them so much?

Facts
Below are some possible reasons.

① Original Sentences

② Original Sentences

Punch Lines
Go fight, beetles!

Hints for Original Sentences

❶ They look like samurai warriors.

❷ They look like superheroes.

❸ It's exciting to find them in the forest.

❹ A championship fighting match is exciting. You can give your beetles some special training.

Writing Time

1 男の子がカブトムシとクワガタムシを大好きな理由を2つ考えて ① と ② に文を入れて、全文を書こう。

Catchy Sentences

Facts

Punch Lines

2 上で書いた文を見ないで書いて、見ないで言おう。

Catchy Sentences

Facts

Punch Lines

Food 〈食べもの〉
Rice Balls
おにぎり

Sample Sentences

Catchy Sentences: Rice balls are Japanese people's comfort food. Even in foreign countries, many athletes must have rice balls to win their games.

Facts: Here're some things you need to know about rice balls.

1. Original Sentences
2. Original Sentences

Punch Lines: No rice balls, no Japanese life!

Hints for Original Sentences

❶ You need rice, salt, and seaweed.

❷ Usually you put something in the middle, for example, grilled salmon, pickled plums (umeboshi), or dried bonito flakes (okaka).

❸ You make a ball / a triangle / an oval.

❹ You wrap each one in plastic wrap or aluminum foil.

Writing Time

1 おにぎりについて 2 つ考えて ①　　 と ②　　 に文を入れて、全文を書こう。

Catchy Sentences

Facts

Punch Lines

2 上で書いた文を見ないで書いて、見ないで言おう。

Catchy Sentences

Facts

Punch Lines

Places 〈場所〉

Shopping Malls
ショッピングモール

音声がきけます♪

Sample Sentences

Catchy Sentences: Shopping malls are the center of everyday life for many Japanese people.

Facts: Nowadays, big shopping malls have many different kinds of businesses.

① Original Sentences

② Original Sentences

Punch Lines: I'd love to live in a shopping mall.

Hints for Original Sentences

❶ There might be a public bath.

❷ There might be a small park with a cafe.

❸ There might be an art gallery.

❹ There might be movie theaters.

Writing Time

1 大型ショッピングモールにあるかもしれないものを2つ考えて ① と ② に文を入れて、全文を書こう。

- Catchy Sentences
- Facts
- Punch Lines

2 上で書いた文を見ないで書いて、見ないで言おう。

- Catchy Sentences
- Facts
- Punch Lines

Nature 〈自然〉

Snow
雪

音声がきけます♪

Sample Sentences

Catchy Sentences

The amount of snowfall in Japan varies from zero centimeters to more than 300 centimeters. It depends on the areas where people live.

Facts

People have different feelings about snow.

① Original Sentences

② Original Sentences

Punch Lines

Dogs and children love snow!

Hints for Original Sentences

❶ Let's go snowboarding.

❷ Hot springs in the snow are the best.

❸ No more snow, please.

❹ Snow is beautiful to look at.

Writing Time

1 雪について思うことを2つ考えて ①___ と ②___ に文を入れて、全文を書こう。

Catchy Sentences

Facts

Punch Lines

2 上で書いた文を見ないで書いて、見ないで言おう。

Catchy Sentences

Facts

Punch Lines

Food 〈食べもの〉

Takoyaki
たこ焼き

Sample Sentences

Catchy Sentences: According to a survey of what foreign tourists like to eat in Japan, takoyaki is number one in Osaka.

Facts: See below for what you need to make homemade takoyaki.

① Original Sentences

② Original Sentences

Punch Lines: If you eat more than 20, you might feel pretty bad afterwards.

Hints for Original Sentences

❶ You need flour, eggs, cabbage, octopus, and pickled ginger.

❷ You need a takoyaki pan.

❸ For topping, you might want powdered seaweed, mayonnaise, and dried bonito flakes.

❹ You need the best takoyaki sauce.

Writing Time

1 家でたこ焼きを作る時に必要なものを2つ考えて ① と ② に文を入れて、全文を書こう。

- Catchy Sentences
- Facts
- Punch Lines

2 上で書いた文を見ないで書いて、見ないで言おう。

- Catchy Sentences
- Facts
- Punch Lines

Living Things 〈生きもの〉

Toki
トキ

音声がきけます♪

Sample Sentences

Catchy Sentences: Once wild Toki were extinct in Japan. But now the number is increasing.

Facts: Toki are important for the following reasons.

① Original Sentences

② Original Sentences

Punch Lines: Someday, hundreds of Toki might fly in our skies again.

Hints for Original Sentences

❶ Toki are the symbols of peaceful Japan.

❷ The beautiful Toki color comes from the birds.

❸ There used to be hundreds of Toki in the Edo period.

❹ Toki survive only in good natural environments.

Writing Time

1 トキについて2つ考えて ① と ② に文を入れて、全文を書こう。

Catchy Sentences

Facts

Punch Lines

2 上で書いた文を見ないで書いて、見ないで言おう。

Catchy Sentences

Facts

Punch Lines

History 〈歴史〉

Tutankhamen
ツタンカーメン

音声がきけます♪

Sample Sentences

Catchy Sentences: I want to interview Tutankhamen, of Egypt. He was an Egyptian pharaoh of the 18th dynasty.

Facts: By using modern CT scan technology on his mummy, it was found that he was about 165 centimeters tall and around 19 years old when he died. Here're my questions.

1. Original Sentences

2. Original Sentences

Punch Lines: I hope he's as good-looking as his golden mask!

Hints for Original Sentences

❶ Why were you buried in a golden coffin?

❷ How did you feel when you became a king at only nine years old?

❸ Why did you die at the age of 19?

❹ What did you eat every day?

Writing Time

1 ツタンカーメンに質問してみたいことを2つ考えて ① と ② に文を入れて、全文を書こう。

- Catchy Sentences
- Facts
- Punch Lines

2 上で書いた文を見ないで書いて、見ないで言おう。

- Catchy Sentences
- Facts
- Punch Lines

Art 〈芸術〉

Van Gogh
ゴッホ

音声がきけます♪

Sample Sentences

Catchy Sentences
Vincent Van Gogh is one of the greatest artists in history. People finally realized he was a genius only after he died.

Facts
Van Gogh's paintings attract many people's attention. Here're some reasons for that.

① Original Sentences

② Original Sentences

Punch Lines
Genius is timeless.

Hints for Original Sentences

❶ He had a dramatic life.

❷ His paintings are so energetic.

❸ His brother supported him well.

Theodorus Van Gogh

❹ He sketched so much beautiful scenery.

Writing Time

1 ゴッホの絵が多くの人の注目を集める理由を 2 つ考えて ① と ② に文を入れて、全文を書こう。

Catchy Sentences

Facts

Punch Lines

2 上で書いた文を見ないで書いて、見ないで言おう。

Catchy Sentences

Facts

Punch Lines

コードを読み取れない方や音声をダウンロードしたい方は、右のQRコードまたは以下のURLより、アクセスしてください。
https://www.mpi-j.co.jp/contents/shop/mpi/contents/digital/tagaki40.html

TAGAKI® 40

発 行 日	2018年10月11日 初版第1刷　2023年1月20日 初版第12刷
	2025年2月1日　2版第2刷
執　　　筆	松香洋子
執 筆 協 力	近藤理恵子
英 文 校 正	Glenn McDougall
編　　　集	株式会社カルチャー・プロ
イ ラ ス ト	鹿野理恵子　メイ ボランチ
本文デザイン	DB Works
本 文 組 版	株式会社内外プロセス
録 音・編 集	一般財団法人英語教育協議会（ELEC）
ナレーション	Howard Colefield　Julia Yermakov
写 真 提 供	新華社　アフロ
協　　　力	赤松由梨　粕谷みゆき　貞野浩子　野中美恵　宮下いづみ　山内由紀子
印　　　刷	シナノ印刷株式会社
発　　　行	株式会社mpi松香フォニックス
	〒151-0053
	東京都渋谷区代々木2-16-2 第二甲田ビル 2F
	fax:03-5302-1652
	URL:https://www.mpi-j.co.jp

不許複製　All rights reserved.
©2018 mpi Matsuka Phonics inc.
ISBN 978-4-89643-748-5

＊本書で取り扱っている内容は、2017年までの情報をもとに作成しています。
＊QRコードは(株)デンソーウェーブの登録商標です。